Triumph over
everything by the
infinite power of
Jesus Christ.

spiritual
technology

Peter John Brooks

Print ISBN 978-1-968804-07-7

Digital ISBN 978-1-968804-06-0

Published by Fivestone New Media

www.bethelcornerstone.org

Contents

technology: *a capability given by the practical application of knowledge*

Merriam-Webster Dictionary

Introduction

Greater is he who is in you than he who is in the world.

1 John 4:4b

THE ROOTS of the world's problems are spiritual, and spiritual problems require spiritual solutions. Jesus Christ demolished sin through his death and resurrection. He poured out the Holy Spirit, making the riches of heaven freely available to everyone who believes in him. The Holy Spirit is the most powerful being in the entire universe (for he is God himself), and he lives inside each child of God. The Holy Spirit can do anything, for with God nothing is impossible.

God does not redeem the world through material technology. He does not inspire faster semiconductors for laptops or better apps for smartphones in order to expand his kingdom. Instead, God works by spiritual power to accomplish his plans on the earth. This is how he worked through Jesus and his apostles, and it's how he works through his people today. The potential power of a human filled with God dwarfs the power of the fastest computer.

Through the Holy Spirit, eternal life, immortality, and full restoration of the creation are possible.

God is waiting for us. He expects us to take the awesome power of the Holy Spirit, go out into the world, confront challenges, and resolve real problems with the authority and love of Jesus. Through a pure revelation of spiritual power, the creation will be set free.

We need to be spiritual people, led by the Spirit, filled with the Spirit, and empowered by the Spirit. Through the operation of the Holy Spirit through the people of God, God's kingdom is going to come, and his will is going to be done, on earth as it is in heaven.

The church is the seat of God's awesome spiritual power on the earth. God lives in his church, and through the church God wants to reveal his power in ever-increasing measure.

C.H. Spurgeon said:

> It is in and through the church that for the present the power of the Messiah is known. Jehovah has given to Jesus all authority in the midst of his people, whom he rules with his royal sceptre, and this power goes forth with divine energy from the church for the ingathering of the elect, and the subduing of all evil. We have need to pray for the sending out of the rod of divine strength. It was by his rod that Moses smote the Egyptians, and wrought wonders for Israel, and even so whenever the Lord Jesus sends forth the rod of his strength, our spiritual enemies are overcome.... We look for the clearer manifestation of his almighty power in the latter days. (Spurgeon, *The Treasury of David*)

These are the last days. God is looking for skillful spiritual workers who will endeavor with him through the power of the Holy Spirit to accomplish his grand purposes on the earth. God wants holy spiritual power to burst out of the prayer closets of his chosen people into the public spaces of the world, revealing his glory and bringing real transformation.

Material technology is insufficient to accomplish God's goals. We need the power of the Holy Spirit. It's time for God's children to learn how to operate spiritual technology. When they do, the limitations of material technology will be overcome by the infinite power of God, and the information age will be replaced by the age of the Holy Spirit.

Chapter 1
Technology from Man or Power from God

WE ARE ACCUSTOMED to material technology, and almost everywhere we turn, we use it. We pop toast in the toaster and get cold milk out of the refrigerator. We enjoy heat in the winter and cool in the summer - all at the touch of a button. We communicate with those far away using mobile phones. Our bodies are healed with medical treatment. We entertain our bored minds with movies and video games, and then we hop in the car and drive across town. Technology permeates our lives. Using it has become as normal as wearing shoes.

Material technology is transforming the earth. It is improving our communications, speeding our transportation, and lengthening our lives. The results are all around us – faster computers, smarter phones, better medicines. Technology keeps pushing out farther, expanding the boundaries of the human experience. Emerging technologies like artificial intelligence, robotics, and gene editing are poised to revolutionize the planet.

The Silicon Valley visionaries who develop these technologies dream big. They believe that material technology holds the key to the world's future. They hope that technology will possibly liberate humanity from all problems. With improved technology, they believe that complete happiness, social utopia, and possibly even eternal life are just around the corner.

Where does our insatiable drive for more and more technology come from?

Technology originates in the simple fact that humanity faces problems, and technology is used to solve these problems. For example, milk spoils when it gets warm, so refrigerators were developed. Cooking food over open fires is hard, so electric ovens and ranges were developed. Technology pumps our water, grows our food, and transports our resources. Technology has addressed many of the world's most pressing problems like lack of clean water, hunger, poverty, and disease.

Technology expands because people seek to solve more problems. The ever-expanding boundaries of technology overcome an increasing array of human problems, as technology promises to make life easier, safer, and happier for everyone.

For most people, technology appears to be a necessary adjunct to human happiness, and it's hard to imagine life without it.

But technology wasn't always a part of this world.

Eden

In the Garden of Eden, there was no material technology. This was not because Adam and Eve were hopelessly primitive, but because everything in Eden was perfect. There was no sickness, so there was no need for medicine. There was no conflict, so there was no need for spears, guns, or bombs. There were no gaps of communication or information, so the internet was not needed. In the Garden of Eden, there was no problem, sickness, pain, sorrow, curse, or lack. Everything was perfect. Adam and Eve were in perfect harmony with each other and with God, and through the Holy Spirit they had everything that they needed. They had no need for material technology because there were no problems to solve. The Holy Spirit took care of everything.

Technology is a way to solve problems. If there are no problems, there is no need for technology.

Fall

Eden's idyll was brief.

Adam sinned by disobeying God, and problems began to rush into the world like air into a failed vacuum tube. Adam and Eve were expelled from the Garden, and they suddenly faced problems on every side. Lack of food became a problem. No longer were delicious fruits hanging in abundance from every tree, ripe for the picking. The cursed ground, reflecting the corruption of sin, began yielding thorns and thistles. Weeds took over. Adam had to work hard to grow grain and coax food out of the earth. Large animals, no longer tame and friendly, suddenly became aggressive and threatening. Satan, no longer held powerless by the holiness of Adam and Eve, gained power to disturb and destroy. Lack of health became a problem - no longer was eternal life guaranteed. Suddenly there was sickness, pain, conflict, sorrow, and decay. Death began its cruel reign. God's beautiful creation began to groan in pain under the bondage of sin.

Centuries passed, families grew, and cultures spread all over the world. Each nation grappled with the inheritance of sin and how to overcome its evil results.

Redemption from sin and its evil effects became the great need of humanity. How can we get food? How will we get clothes? How will we heal our bodies? How can we heal our relationships? Where will we find peace of mind?

All over the world, humanity cried out for the things that had been broken by sin and left behind in Eden. They cried out for redemption.

Redemption by Technology

Most cultures quickly discovered that the quickest, most reliable way to solve problems was through material technology. Stone hunting tools were developed. Pottery spread, and metallurgy became popular. As basic as these primitive technologies were, they made survival easier in a world screaming with problems. Technology alleviated some of the harmful results of the Fall.

Today, technology advances exponentially. The problem of food eventually brought forth the plow, which has morphed into tractors and large motorized equipment. Today, complex grain mills, hydroponics, and other advanced technologies alleviate the sweat of the brow required to get food (see Gen. 3:19).

The problem of sickness led to the development of medical technology. Today, herbs and poultices have been replaced by robotic surgery and powerful drugs. The need for psychological repair has led to medications that soothe troubled minds. People need to travel long distances, so horse-drawn carriages were used, which gave way to cars and airplanes. People wanted to communicate with others far away, so the telegraph was invented. The dashes and dots of Morse Code were soon replaced by the telephone, which in turn is being supplanted by video-calling.

The Bible says that the last enemy facing humanity is death (see 1 Corinthians 15:26). Silicon Valley entrepreneurs are now trying to conquer this final, dread frontier. Wealthy visionaries are seeking to eradicate death and enable people to live forever. Some believe the union of humanity with computers will enable people to have eternal life within a century (see, for example, *Fantastic Voyage* by Ray Kurzweil).

Wild dreams like this no longer seem crazy. Faith in technology appears to be justified, as humanity has experienced its salvation in many aspects of life. Loved ones have been saved from disease by antibiotics. Relationships have been maintained over the miles through the internet. People survive freezing temperatures because of central heating, feed their children with packaged food, and fly in airplanes across the world.

There is no doubt that technology has accomplished amazing things. It has redeemed the world from some problems.

But God has a better way of redemption.

Redemption by God

God's way of redeeming the world is through his Son Jesus Christ. All redemption is possible through the Son of God. Jesus healed with a touch of his hand (Matthew 8:14). He multiplied provision for hungry thousands (Matthew 14:17-20). He created a coin in a fish for a disciple who needed to pay his taxes (Matthew 17:27). Jesus brought peace to troubled minds and restored terrible sinners to God. He expelled demons with a word. He even stopped a funeral procession and raised up a dead man (Luke 7:11-17). Christ revealed perfect redemption from heaven, and this spiritual power astounded the world. People had never seen anything like it before.

Jesus came primarily for souls, to rescue them, set them free, and plant them in heaven. But he redeemed bodies, minds, and circumstances too. He healed the sick, raised the dead, expelled demons, brought peace, and multiplied provision. As Jesus walked the earth, multifaceted redemption followed him wherever he went.

Superiority of Spiritual Redemption

When Jesus came to town, people rushed to him for solutions to their problems, and they forgot about other redemptive tools. It was obvious that Jesus' redemption was fuller, more perfect, and more complete than any other. Imagine a technology that could solve your every problem, sort out your every issue, heal all your diseases, take away all your depression, and make you live forever. This is the salvation of Jesus.

Jesus came to a world that was accustomed to improving technological tools in order to solve problems— like making better clay pots, improving knives, or making stronger adobe walls. Jesus didn't work on any of these things. He never focused on improving material technology. Jesus redeemed the world with spiritual power.

When Peter's mother-in-law was sick with a fever, Jesus didn't send her to the local herbal compounder along with an idea for more effective medication. He touched her hand, and the fever left. When he had 5,000 people to feed, he didn't rush to the bakery, improving their production line to churn out more buns. He made loaves out of thin air. When Peter's boat was in a storm, Jesus didn't give him tips on how to improve the boat's performance, tweaking the stern or adjusting the sails. He called Peter out of his boat to walk on the water.

Jesus didn't pursue material technology. He pursued God. He never emphasized improving material technology. He emphasized the work of the Holy Spirit. If someone was sick, Jesus healed that person through prayer. If a crowd was hungry, he multiplied loaves. If someone was demonized, he cast out the demon. Jesus offered spiritual solutions for the redemption of humanity that perfectly addressed all problems humanity could possibly face.

Material technology is the primary way of practical redemption for us today, but it was of little interest to Jesus. This doesn't mean he thought material technology was bad. It just means he had a better way. Material technology might alleviate the symptoms, but it will never cure the ultimate disease. All problems in the world are from the spiritual root of sin. If these problems are to be resolved, the root of sin must be destroyed. This is why Jesus went to the cross, destroying the spiritual root of human problems and bringing in eternal, permanent salvation that affects all aspects of life.

If Jesus were on the earth today, he would work no differently than he did 2,000 years ago. Material technology is more advanced today, but Jesus wouldn't change. To feed a crowd, Jesus would do the same thing he did in Galilee. He wouldn't carry a laptop, connect to artificial intelligence in the cloud, and advise an e-commerce company on how to perfect drone delivery so he could buy buns from the nearest bakery. Instead, he would consult with his Father and offer the simple solution of creating something out of nothing. That's easier, faster, and glorifies God. The work of the Holy Spirit is timeless, perfect, and complete. It's God's way of redeeming the world. It's why Jesus came.

The Spiritual Rules the Material

Material technology cannot redeem the world. It is limited, confined by materials and natural laws. Material technology depends on the fact that A+B=C, yesterday, today, and tomorrow; in the air, under the ground, and on the moon. Repeatable, reliable laws of chemistry and physics define the boundaries within which material technology operates. Material technology can never go outside of these boundaries. The law of gravity, the laws of thermodynamics, physical laws of mass and motion, and the laws of chemistry are some of the fixed laws that define the boundaries of material technology.

Jesus has no such limitations. He operates outside natural laws. He wrote them all. He does not depend upon them; they depend upon him. He is not confined by them; they are confined by him. He precedes natural laws, will outlast them, is superior to them, and undergirds them. The material world came into existence by the word of God, and God's word upholds the world until now.

Jesus is the Word of God. The word of God is the foundational reality of the universe. When a foundation moves, the thing on top of it moves too. When God speaks, things in the earth obey him. Chemical reactions bow to the one who defines the way that chemicals and molecules interact. Physical reality bends when faced with the one who defines the laws of mass and motion.

How can someone turn 5 loaves into 5,000? It can only happen through spiritual power. Even with the most advanced material technology, such feats are impossible. Scientists can never create something out of nothing. But God can do it. He did so with the entire universe in the beginning, and he can do so again now.

The working of the Holy Spirit is superior to material technology because it's faster, easier, and simpler. Speak, and the result comes. Touch someone, and healing happens. Did your excited friend cut off someone's ear? No need to rush to the hospital for stitches and antibiotics. Just reattach the ear with your hand (Luke 22:50-51). Pray, and food multiplies. Get rid of cancer by a command. The Holy Spirit offers full redemption for any situation.

For Jesus, miracles are not a last resort when material technology fails. Miraculous power is his main plan. Through the operation of spiritual technology, Jesus proved that with God all things are possible.

The Full Victory of Christ

Jesus perfectly addressed every problem that humanity faces. God wanted all evil removed from the world, and Jesus made it possible. His redemptive wake left nothing undone.

Through the cross, Jesus conquered the Fall. He shed his blood to pay the price of sin, and then he rose up again, breaking the power of hell. Resurrection proved that his payment was sufficient, and that he had once for all taken away the sins of the world. Jesus cut down sin, the tree of all trouble, and he took away every problem that grows out of this noxious root. Satan was destroyed, demonic powers were defeated, sickness was eliminated, death was done away with, and the curse was reversed. All that was lost through Adam was recovered through Christ.

Christ rose up from the dead, after shouting, "It is finished," and brought the full redemption of the kingdom of God with him. When he poured out the Holy Spirit on the Day of Pentecost, he opened up a portal for heaven to flow down into the earth and bring full salvation, redemption, and perfect deliverance all over the world.

Through his death and resurrection, Jesus bought the right for Eden to be restored to the earth.

- RECAP -

1. There were no problems in Eden, so there was no material technology.

2. When sin came, so did problems.

3. Material technology is a way to solve problems and redeem people from the evil effects of the Fall.

4. The redemption offered by material technology is limited because it is based on matter and material laws, and it doesn't address the root problem of sin.

5. Jesus is God's plan for redemption for the broken world. His redemption is complete because it addresses the spiritual problem of sin which is the root of all material problems.

- PRAYER -

Heavenly Father, thank you for how you created the world - perfect in every way. Evil came in, but your Son Jesus is strong enough to take it all away. I believe that Jesus is the only real and permanent solution for the evil in this world. Your redemption is perfect, and you are strong enough to resolve every problem. Open my eyes to see the full extent of your redemption. Help me believe in your ability to impact every single challenge with your power. Let me not limit you. In Jesus' name I pray. Amen.

Chapter 2
Spiritual Technology in the Bible

Miracles are a retelling in small letters of the very same story which is written across the whole world in letters too large for some of us to see.

C.S. Lewis, *God In The Dock*

SPIRITUAL TECHNOLOGY is *the application of spiritual knowledge resulting in a manifestation of divine spiritual power.* Spiritual technology is heaven coming into the earth; it is God impacting our world by his Holy Spirit. Spiritual technology is similar to material technology except it uses gifts from the Holy Spirit in order to accomplish things on the earth.

Spiritual technology is the most powerful form of technology, because it comes from God. Like God, it has no limits. It can work anywhere, in any place. It can do anything God wants it to do. It can have material results - affecting matter, and it can have spiritual results - affecting the spiritual realm.

When Jesus healed a blind man, he didn't use a scalpel and surgical procedure; he used spiritual power. The Holy Spirit restored the cornea and retina and every other part of his eye. That is spiritual technology.

Spiritual technology is God's modus operandi - it's the way he operates. God is a Spirit, and he works through spiritual power to solve problems. When someone is born again, a dead human spirit is made alive. Raising a dead human spirit to eternal life is probably the greatest miracle possible. This work, like many of the most important works in the world, can only happen by the Holy Spirit.

Miracles are normal for God. God's work is miraculous because God is miraculous; he's beyond nature and above natural laws.

Miracles come from heaven.

In the Bible, the word "heaven" does not describe a physical location in outer space. It refers to the spiritual realm where God lives.

Miracles impact the earth.

Earth is the material realm where we live. "Heaven is my throne, and earth is my footstool," God says (Isa. 66:1). God made the earth, and he is the supreme authority over it. It belongs to him, and he can do anything he wants on it. Whenever God acts on the earth, manipulating matter, miracles happen.

God wants heaven to dominate the earth. Heaven dominates the earth through divine spiritual power. When miracles happen, heaven rules.

The Bible testifies to the infinite power and possibilities of spiritual technology, giving many examples of its purpose and use. Throughout history, godly men and women have utilized spiritual technology in order to glorify God and manifest his power upon the earth. Examples of spiritual technology abound throughout the Old and New Testaments, from the beginning of the Bible to the end of the Bible. It's how the prophets worked in the Old Testament, it's how Jesus worked when he walked the earth, and it's how his disciples worked after he rose up to heaven and poured out the Holy Spirit. Biblical examples of spiritual technology prove that the Spirit of God is able to meet every need and solve every problem that came into the world through the Fall. The spiritual technology that operated in the Bible is still available for God's people today.

Let's look at some of the many different ways spiritual technology operated in the Bible.

Provision

A poor widow had a small jar of flour and a little oil. Starvation threatened her household. Elijah gave her instructions, and she obeyed. She made what she thought would be her last meal, but to her surprise, as she used up her precious ingredients, more of them appeared. She just couldn't use them up. Her little jars of oil and flour never emptied out, being constantly re-filled with supernatural supply (1 Kings 17:8-16).

Elisha prayed for another woman, and a small pot of olive oil turned into many gallons. She sold off the extra oil to pay off all her debts and provide for her family (2 Kings 4:1-7). (Good olive oil is expensive, especially if it's straight from God, and this miracle might have left the woman wealthy.)

During a famine, Elisha multiplied a little food to feed a large group of people. This foreshadowed the food-multiplication miracles of Jesus (2 Kings 4:42-44).

Jesus multiplied bread and fish on at least two occasions, once turning a boy's meal into enough food for many thousands (Mark 6:35-44 and Mark 8:1-9). He taught us again and again that we need not be limited by our natural supply. God is all we need.

Jesus promises to provide food and clothing to those who seek first his kingdom and his righteousness (Matthew 6:33). Even if Jesus has to work miracles to take care of us, he's going to keep his word.

Information and Intelligence Gathering

Through the Holy Spirit, the blind prophet Ahijah knew who his visitors were and why they had come to him, before they came near his door (1 Kings 14:5).

Peter had divine revelation about visitors before they came (Acts 10:19-20).

Elisha was accustomed to receiving knowledge about his visitors, and he was surprised once when God didn't tell him who they were (2 Kings 4:27).

These men didn't need video cameras at their doors connected to their smartphones, because they had regular revelation from the Holy Spirit.

God told Elisha about the movements of the enemy's army (2 Kings 6:8-12). Spiritual spying rescued the Israelite army on more than one occasion. They didn't need a satellite system or a radar because they had military intelligence from God.

Isaiah, Jeremiah, Ezekiel, Daniel, and many other prophets knew what would happen in the future because God told them. John saw what would happen more than 2,000 years before it did, and he recorded his discoveries in the book of Revelation.

Peter knew when people were lying to him (Acts 5:1-3). He didn't need to hire detectives because he was in touch with God, who knows everything.

When the early Christians prophesied, secrets hidden in the hearts of unbelievers were exposed (1 Corinthians

14:24-25). With technology like this, the early church didn't need to run background checks.

Spiritually Seeing Things from a Distance

Through the Spirit, Elisha saw his servant Gehazi go and take a gift from Naaman the Syrian (2 Kings 5:25-26).

By spiritual means, Jesus saw his future disciple Nathaniel sitting under a fig tree in another place (John 1:48).

Paul, through the Spirit, saw the meetings of the church in Colosse (Colossians 2:5).

Seeing events far away through the Spirit is more effective than the most advanced forms of videoconferencing.

Transportation

Elijah was regularly transported by the Spirit of God from one place to another (1 Kings 18:12; 2 Kings 2:16). He didn't need cars, buses, or trains. God just picked him up and put him where he wanted him to be.

Ezekiel was lifted up physically from one place and deposited in another place where there were people who needed to hear the word of God (Ezekiel 3:14-15).

Jesus didn't need a boat, but he walked on water (Mark 6:48).

Philip was caught away from one place to another, physically transported by the Holy Spirit (Acts 8:39-40). He was one minister who didn't need a private airplane.

Iron Floating

Once an axe head fell into the water. Elisha made it float so someone could pull it out (2 Kings 6:5). That was a helpful technique, especially since this particular axe head was borrowed.

Invisibility

Jesus, when he was chased by persecutors, became invisible and walked right through the midst of them (John 8:59). Today, companies are trying to develop invisibility cloaks, but Jesus mastered this technology 2,000 years ago by the Holy Spirit.

Stopping Witchcraft

Paul cast a demon out of a fortune-teller by the power of God (Acts 16:18). Witchcraft has no power against a true servant of God.

Health

Elisha miraculously removed poison from a pot of soup (2 Kings 4:39-41).

Sarah had a child after she entered menopause (Gen. 18:10-11; 21:2).

Elijah healed Naaman from leprosy (2 Kings 5:14).

Jesus healed the sick. Healing was a fundamental part of his ministry. Everyone who came to him was healed. Entire towns were emptied of all of their sick people when Jesus came to visit (Matthew 4:24, 8:16-17; Luke 4:40). Jesus died on the cross not only to take away our sins, but to take away our physical sicknesses (compare Matthew 8:16-17 and Isaiah 53:4-5).

Peter and John regularly healed sick people (Acts 3:1-11; 9:33-34).

Radical life-extension is easy for the Holy Spirit. After all, Methuselah lived 969 years.

If that much healing went on today, doctors, hospitals, and drug companies would lose a lot of business.

Protection From Mobs

Violent homosexuals seeking to rape men at Lot's house were struck blind by the power of God (Genesis 19:11).

Jesus was dragged to the edge of a cliff by a mob, but he rendered them powerless. He walked right through the midst of them (Luke 4:29-30).

An armed mob came to arrest Jesus at midnight, but he spoke two words and they all fell down backwards (John 18:6).

Mobs can be very intimidating. But God's power is greater.

Weather Modification

Today there are attempts to control the weather, through cloud-seeding or other technologies. But this is easy for God.

Elijah prayed and stopped rain for 3.5 years (James 5:17).

Jesus stopped storms and stilled rough seas by speaking to them (Matthew 8:26).

Warfare

When fleeing Egypt, the army of Pharaoh chased after the children of Israel. God split a sea, allowing them to pass through on dry land. When the Egyptians tried to cross through, God covered them with the water, and they drowned (Hebrews 11:29).

Elisha, when surrounded by the army of Syria, struck the soldiers blind by the power of God and led them into captivity (2 Kings 6:18-20).

Throughout the Old Testament, the army of Israel experienced miraculous deliverance and victory on multiple occasions. Spiritual power can stop an army of any size and render any military technology impotent. It can blunt spears. It can make fighter planes useless. It can disarm bombs.

Conquest of Death

The widow's son at Nain, a cold corpse in the midst of a funeral procession, came back to life when Jesus touched the coffin (Luke 7:11-15).

Jesus raised Lazarus back to life after he had been dead for 3 days and had begun to decompose (John 11:39-44).

Jesus' disciples raised people from the dead. Dorcas died and was ready to be buried, but Peter touched her, and she came back to life (Acts 9:36-41).

Paul, when stoned and left for dead, got up again (Acts 14:19-20).

Paul raised up the dead body of a young man who fell down to his death after becoming sleepy during one of his long messages (Acts 20:9-10).

Even in the Old Testament, God's servants raised people back to life. Elijah once raised up a dead boy (2 Kings 4:32-35).

Needless to say, if someone can conquer death, they are completely unstoppable.

Conclusion

There are infinite possibilities through the Holy Spirit. If God's people can believe his word and obey him, they can do anything. This is the testimony of the entire Bible.

The Old Testament rings with miracles. But now in the New Covenant, should not the operations of spiritual technology today surpass the greatest miracles of the Old Testament? Christ has come, his Spirit is inside believers, and they have become parts of his body. Jesus said the least believer is greater than the greatest Old Testament prophet (Matthew 11:11)!

We should expect miracles! Miracles are not the goal of our faith; the glory of God is, but when miracles happen, God is glorified. If we want God's glory to come, we should pray like the early church did, "Grant that signs and wonders may be done!" (Acts 4:30).

Spiritual technology was not a temporary measure for a special time. It's not as though the world needed miracles in those days because material technology was so primitive, but today advanced computers and hospitals have taken over, so miracles are no longer necessary. No way!

Material technology cannot finish what the Holy Spirit started.

Spiritual power is the way God works in the earth. He will continue to work this way until his glory is revealed all over the world, and the age is finished.

Throughout history, God's people have faced great challenges. The only real solution to these challenges has been the operation of spiritual technology. We are heading into a challenging time in the future, and only by the power of the Holy Spirit will we be able to stand.

- RECAP -

1. Spiritual technology is the application of spiritual knowledge resulting in manifestations of divine spiritual power.

2. Spiritual technology is Biblical. The Bible is full of people operating spiritual technology.

3. Through divine spiritual technology, nothing is impossible.

- PRAYER -

Father, thank you for how you work in the earth through your Holy Spirit. You can do anything. For you, the supernatural is normal. Thank you that I am surrounded by your miracles. My life is a miracle. The Holy Spirit inside me is a miracle! I acknowledge that you have chosen spiritual power as your means of transforming this world. Father, your ways are perfect. Open my eyes to see that your Holy Spirit is able to resolve every problem that I could ever face. Help me to walk with you and see your miracles happen. In Jesus' name I pray. Amen.

Chapter 3
Revelation, Faith, Obedience: Releasing God's Power

Forgive me for being so ordinary while claiming to know so extraordinary a God.

Jim Elliot

IT IS POSSIBLE for every Christian to release the most potent force in the world - the power of Almighty God.

Most assuredly, I say to you, he who believes in me, the works that I do he will do also, and greater works than these he will do, because I go to my Father. (John 14:12)

Read those words of Jesus again.

> Most assuredly, I say to you, he who believes in me, the works that I do he will do also, and greater works than these he will do, because I go to my Father. (John 14:12)

If you're a believer in Jesus, you can do the same miracles that Jesus did. You can operate spiritual technology just like Jesus did. This is God's will! God has called you to a supernatural life. Every born-again believer has the potential to heal the sick, prophesy, cast out demons, and even raise the dead. Even greater miracles are possible because God is inside you. This calling is for every Christian. With God, there are no limits!

God wants to work miracles through his people. He wants the world to see the awesome power of his name!

Awake from the limitations of unbelief. The operation of spiritual technology depends on the Holy Spirit, not on ourselves.

Miracles are a normal part of true Christianity because the Holy Spirit is the normal power of true Christianity. Where the Holy Spirit is working, supernatural power will operate. We can be bold and strong conquerors for God because the Holy Spirit is inside us. With the awesome resources of heaven available to us, we ought to see the power of God's kingdom revealed!

Jesus told us, "With men this is impossible, but with God all things are possible" (Matthew 19:26). There is no situation that is beyond the reach and ability of Almighty God.

Practical Spirituality

True spirituality is practical. It does not hide in a cloistered corner, but it goes out into the streets of the world, boldly and humbly influencing people with the gospel. True faith obtains a testimony because it has demonstrable results. God wants our faith in him to be *practiced*, so through us he can achieve his earthly goals.

Practical Christianity means operating by the Holy Spirit. It means using spiritual technology to tap into the infinite resources of God in order to resolve earthly problems in order to glorify God. It means practically manifesting the redemptive power of Jesus into a broken world and healing it through the gospel.

To have practical spirituality, we need to learn how to operate spiritual technology.

Baptism of the Holy Spirit

First, in order to operate spiritual technology, we need to be baptized in the Holy Spirit. Each child of God receives the Holy Spirit when he or she is born again (see Ephesians 1:13-14), but we're not automatically baptized in the Holy Spirit.

Jesus said:

> John truly baptized with water, but you shall be baptized with the Holy Spirit not many days from now... you shall receive power when the Holy Spirit has come upon you; and you shall be witnesses to Me. (Acts 2:5-8a)

These disciples were already born again and had the Holy Spirit inside them (John 20:22). They believed in Jesus, for they saw him resurrected. But they needed to be baptized in the Holy Spirit in order to fulfill their calling.

Being born again is not the same as being baptized in the Holy Spirit. As D. Martyn Lloyd-Jones said, "You can be a believer, that you can have the Holy Spirit dwelling in you, and still not be baptized with the Holy Spirit" (Lloyd-Jones, *Joy Unspeakable*).

The baptism of the Holy Spirit happens when a believer is filled with the Holy Spirit for the first time. This baptism bestows spiritual gifts and imparts power for ministry (Acts 2:4; 8:14-17).

Each believer who wants to fulfill their potential in Christ needs to be baptized in the Holy Spirit.

Once D.L. Moody had some Bible teachers at his school who didn't believe in the baptism in the Holy Spirit. Moody profoundly disagreed with them.

> Once he [Moody] had some teachers at Northfield – fine men, all of them, but they did not believe in a definite baptism with the Holy Ghost for the individual. They believed that every child of God was baptized with the Holy Ghost, and they did not believe in any special baptism with the Holy Ghost for the individual. Mr. Moody said, "Why don't they see that this is just the one thing that they themselves need? They are good teachers, they are wonderful teachers, and I am so glad to have them here, but why will they not see that the baptism with the Holy Ghost is just the one touch that they themselves?" (R.A. Torrey, *Why God Used D.L. Moody*)

Eventually Moody convinced these men that they needed to be baptized in the Holy Spirit, and they were.

If we're going to operate spiritual technology, we need to be baptized in the Holy Spirit.

Obeying the New Testament

In addition to being baptized in the Holy Spirit, if we're going to operate spiritual technology, we must obey the word of God. The Bible tells us how God wants us to live and what he wants us to do. Obeying the New Testament is essential for operating spiritual technology, because there is no true miracle apart from submission to the word of God.

Bible study is not about increasing intellectual knowledge. It's about learning what God wants us to do so we can obey him and represent him accurately to the world.

After being baptized in the Holy Spirit and purposing to submit completely to the word of God as revealed in the New Testament, there are three simple steps to operating spiritual technology.

Step 1. Get a Revelation

To operate spiritual technology, we need specific revelation from God. We need to know what supernatural work God wants to do through us and when he wants to do it. We can't just use God's power according to our own will. Spiritual technology must always operate according to God's will. We need specific instructions from God regarding when and how to work a miracle.

Revelation means hearing what God is saying specifically to us now and being led by the Holy Spirit. "For as many as are led by the Spirit of God, these are the sons of God" (Rom. 8:14). A son of God brings forth into the world the works of his Father. Being led by the Holy Spirit means receiving communication from the Holy Spirit and following it.

Jesus Lived by Revelation

Jesus lived by revelation. He received specific instructions from his Father about where to go, what to say, and what to do. Whatever he did was authored by his Father. All his words and works originated in God.

"Most assuredly, I say to you, the Son can do nothing of himself, but what he sees the Father do; for whatever he does, the Son also does in like manner" (John 5:19).

Jesus was totally confined to the will of his Father. He laid aside his own will and completely submitted to God. He did nothing until he saw the Father do it, and he said nothing until he heard the Father say it. This is why astounding levels of spiritual technology operated through Jesus.

Jesus and his brothers were different. Once Jesus' brothers asked Jesus to go somewhere with them. Jesus replied, "My time has not yet come, but your time is always ready" (John 7:6b). Jesus' brothers could go wherever they wanted and do what they liked because they were in charge of their own lives. However, this "freedom" came at a price. Since their lives were based on their own authority, they lacked spiritual power. Jesus was different. Jesus could not go with his brothers because his Father didn't tell him to. While his brothers were free to do what they wanted anytime, Jesus had to wait until his Father said he could go.

Jesus didn't try a lot of things just hoping something would work out. Instead, he did the specific things that his Father told him to do. Revelation gave Jesus spiritual precision, which guaranteed that his ministry hit the target every time. Following the leading of the Holy Spirit prevents haphazard religious activity that bears little fruit. Revelation makes ministry powerful.

The Early Church Ministered by Revelation

Throughout the New Testament, the Holy Spirit guided the leaders of the church. They didn't just do what they wanted in ministry. They did what God wanted, basing their ministry on specific revelations from God. They went where God told them to go, did what he told them to do, and spoke what he told them to speak.

There are several examples of how God led the early Christians throughout the New Testament.

> Paul and his companions traveled throughout the region of Phrygia and Galatia, having been kept by the Holy Spirit from preaching the word in the province of Asia. When they came to the border of Mysia, they tried to enter Bithynia, but the Spirit of Jesus would not allow them to. So they passed by Mysia and went down to Troas. During the night, Paul had a vision of a man of Macedonia standing and begging him, 'Come over to Macedonia and help us.' After Paul had seen the vision, we got ready at once to leave for Macedonia, concluding that God had called us to preach the gospel to them. (Acts 16:6-10)

This passage shows how the early church leaders were led by the Holy Spirit. First, the Holy Spirit stopped Paul and his companions from ministering in one area. Then he stopped them from going to another place. Finally, Paul saw a vision of where they were to go, and they went there. Their ministry activities were based on revelation from God, not their own ideas.

This type of ministry is not just for a few apostles like Paul; it's for everyone. True ministry must be based on God's leading. God has specific things he wants each person to do, and we need to find out what these things are by revelation.

Lloyd-Jones explains:

> There is no question but that God's people can look for and expect "leadings", "guidance", indications of what they are meant to do. . . . Men have been told by the Holy Spirit to do something; they knew it was the Holy Spirit speaking to them; and it transpired that it obviously was his leading. (Lloyd-Jones, *The Sovereign Spirit*)

We aren't just supposed to think up a ministry plan and then ask God to bless it. We need to hear from God. Saints throughout history have heard specifically from God and done what he said.

George Muller said, "How important it is to ascertain the will of God, before we undertake anything, because we are then not only blessed in our own souls, but also the work of our hands will prosper." Everything we do in ministry is to be authored by God, and God's specific word is the ground of all true and successful ministry.

"Man shall not live by bread alone, but by every word that proceeds out of the mouth of God" (Matt. 4:4b).

Jesus was not talking about how to live a physical life in this world. He was talking about how to live a healthy spiritual life. He was saying that to really live as God intends, we need to hear what God is saying. When we hear from God, we will be able to live out the life of God upon the earth as we operate spiritual technology.

Pray

To get a revelation from God, we need to pray. Prayer means having a conversation with God. When we pray, we not only talk to God, sharing our hearts and thoughts with him, but we hear from him. God speaks to us during prayer. We are instructed to "pray without ceasing" (1 Thessalonians 5:17). This is so we can be in continual fellowship with our Father and hear what he wants to say.

When he was on the earth, Jesus prayed frequently. Sometimes he spent all night in prayer. During prayer, the Father spoke to him and gave him specific directions. Then Jesus did what the Father wanted. Prayer was the basis for his ministry, because it enabled him to receive revelation from the Father about what to say and do.

Effective Christians throughout history have always been people of prayer, like Jesus was. They grounded their ministry on God's living words, not their own plans. Because of their prayer lives, God could be the source of their ministry and not themselves. For example, Martin Luther said, "I have so much to do today that I shall spend the first three hours in prayer." It should be similar for us.

Hearing from God

Hearing from God is supposed to be normal for Christians. Jesus said, "My sheep hear my voice" (John 10:27a). All born-again believers are God's sheep, and they all can hear God's voice. Each one has received spiritual ears from God so they can hear the Holy Spirit speak to them.

Some Christians have trouble hearing God speak. Just like our physical ears can get blocked, so our spiritual ears can get blocked. There is a solution for this problem. Get out the Bible. The Bible is a sharp spiritual instrument that can cut through the debris that blocks us from hearing from God.

> For the word of God is living and powerful, and sharper than any two-edged sword, piercing even to the division of soul and spirit, and of joints and marrow, and is a discerner of the thoughts and intents of the heart. (Hebrews 4:12)

The Bible opens the ears of God's children so they can hear God speak to them now. When we meditate on the Bible, our spiritual ears are opened and we are able to hear God's voice.

This is why the Bible says, "Hearing [is] by the word of God" (Romans 10:17b). The ability to hear God speak to us now comes as we spend time reading the word of God. The more time we spend meditating on the Bible, the more our spiritual ears will be opened to hear God's voice.

Live in Heaven

When we were born again, God "raised us up together, and made us sit together in the heavenly places in Christ Jesus" (Ephesians 2:6a). Spiritually, we are already in heaven now. All true revelation comes from heaven. To get a revelation, our spiritual eyes and ears need to be opened to see and hear this heavenly environment where our spirits are in Christ with God.

Elijah stood spiritually in heaven even while he was on the earth. "The God, before whom I stand..." (1 Kings 17:1). Elijah's spirit was standing before God in heaven even while his body walked the earth. Out from the presence of God, awesome power flowed forth, as God worked with Elijah to reveal his power to the world.

Jesus also lived spiritually in heaven while he walked upon the earth. He described himself as "the Son of Man who is in heaven" (John 3:13). Jesus was spiritually in heaven while he was on the earth in his body. His Spirit was always in tune with the Father, regardless of where his body was on the earth.

We are called to live the same way. We are heavenly, spiritual people, rescued from this world in order to glorify God. Our citizenship and true home is in heaven, and that is where our spirits already are. We are in the presence of God, hidden in Jesus Christ. We need to live on the basis of our heavenly position, revealing heaven to the world. When we are in fellowship with our Father, hearing his voice and walking with him, we will receive revelations from God.

Testing Revelations

Whenever we believe that God has spoken to us and given us a revelation, we need to test that revelation. We must find out if it's really from God. We are not infallible, and not everything that we initially think is a revelation from God is from God. Sometimes a "revelation" may come from ourselves, from the influence of other people, or from the influence of evil spirits. We must test all revelations. "Test all things; hold fast what is good" (1 Thessalonians 5:21).

The first way to test a revelation is to measure it by the standard of the Bible. Whatever God has spoken will line up with the Bible. Anything that doesn't line up with the Bible is not a word from God. In order to test revelation by the Bible, we need to be familiar with the Bible. Each believer should read through the entire Bible as soon as possible after being born again so that they equip themselves to test revelations by God's word.

We can also test a revelation by getting input from more experienced believers. Mature Christians can help us discern what God might be saying. There are many different gifts in the body of Christ, and some people will be more gifted in some areas than we are. Some will have a gift of discernment, while others will have a stronger ability to hear from God than we do. Bring your revelation to the body of Christ, and see if they confirm what you think you have received from the Lord.

Learning to distinguish God's voice from other voices will take practice. This important skill develops through experience.

Sabbath Rest

Living by revelation will bring us to spiritual rest. Jesus was at perfect rest all the time because he lived by revelation. Sometimes there were terrible storms around him, but he was at rest in God. On a stormy sea, he was able to sleep on the boat even when everyone else was in a panic (Mark 4:37-38). Jesus was at rest because he was always in the center of his Father's will.

Jesus invites us to enter into his rest and experience it for ourselves. "Take My yoke upon you and learn from Me, for I am gentle and lowly in heart, and you will find rest for your souls" (Matthew 11:29). When we take Jesus' yoke upon us, we enter into his plans for our lives. He leads us to fulfill these plans, and his power enables us to accomplish these plans. We find that our life in Christ will become easy because his power is flowing through us.

When we rest in God, we keep the Sabbath. Jesus always kept the Sabbath because he always was at rest in God. The Pharisees thought Jesus was breaking the Sabbath when he healed a man on Saturday, but that wasn't true. Jesus was at perfect rest that Saturday because he saw his Father working, so he also worked. God wanted the man healed, so Jesus healed him.

Jesus sets us free from one-day-a-week Sabbath observance and brings us into the spiritual reality of resting in God all the time.

"So let no one judge you in food or in drink, or regarding a festival or a new moon or sabbaths, which are a shadow of things to come, but the substance is of Christ" (Colossians 2:16-17).

The Sabbath day symbolizes spiritually resting in God, 24 hours a day, 7 days a week. It's a call to stop our own works and do God's works every moment of our lives.

"For he who has entered into his rest has himself also ceased from his works as God did from his" (Hebrews 4:10).

To enter this spiritual Sabbath, we must stop doing our own works and do God's works. We must be willing to end our own ideas and plans for our lives, and seek God for his ideas and plans. We must listen to God and find out what he wants us to do.

Resting in God depends on hearing God's voice. It depends on revelation. "'Today,' after such a long time, as it has been said: 'Today, if you will hear His voice, Do not harden your hearts'" (Hebrews 4:7).

Hearing from God is the way to enter into Sabbath rest. When we hear God speak, we can know his will. When we know his will, we can do his will. When we do God's will, we rest in him.

Eternal Works

When we rest in God, we are not being lazy and doing nothing. Instead, we are doing the specific works that God has prepared for us to do with our lives. This may mean that we are working harder than ever; but we are working in the strength of our Father, not in our own strength.

"For we are His workmanship, created in Christ Jesus for good works, which God prepared beforehand that we should walk in them" (Ephesians 2:10).

God has a specific plan for each believer. He has things that he wants each one of us to accomplish on the earth as long as we are here. He planned for these works at the foundation of the world. In order to find out what these works are, we need to hear from God. These are not our own works that originate in ourselves; they are God's works that originate in him. These are the only works we can do that will have eternal value. When we find out what these works are and do them, we enter into God's rest.

The penalty for breaking the Sabbath in the Old Testament was death. This signifies that when we do our own work instead of God's work, we will not bring life to ourselves or to others. In fact, our own self-effort might bring us and other people down. But when we do God's works, we will have results that bring life.

The starting point for operating spiritual technology is getting a revelation from God.

Step 2. Faith

After receiving a revelation from God, the next step to operating spiritual technology is to have faith. We need to believe that God will do what he said he would do; we must have faith that our revelation from God is going to happen.

According to the Bible, "faith comes by hearing" (Romans 10:17a). When we hear God speak to us, faith arises within us. Faith is a byproduct of hearing from God. Faith sees the invisible things of God (gets a revelation) and believes in those things. Faith trusts the invisible things of heaven more than visible things on the earth. Faith looks to God, sees his word, and believes his word will come to pass. True faith is always based on God's word. This faith is full, substantial, real; and it carries spiritual power.

Empty Faith

Empty faith is not based on God's word, and it has no divine spiritual foundation. It is empty because it has nothing spiritually real to grab onto; it's just based on thin air. Contrary to popular opinion, our faith does not create spiritual reality. Nor can our faith manipulate reality according to our own desires. Real faith is based on a real word from God. It submits to God, sees what God wants to do, and believes he will do it.

An actual revelation of God must precede genuine faith. Someone might go to the hospital and pray for everyone to be healed, having faith that they will all be healed. But without a revelation from God, this faith is empty, and this ministry will fail. Successful ministry begins with receiving an actual revelation from God and believing it. Otherwise, it's not the ministry of God.

We must be willing to wait to get a real revelation from God, and then after getting it, we must wait for God's timing to bring it to pass. Let's not just run out and do our own thing. It's better to do nothing while waiting for God than to rush out and do a lot of things that are not initiated by him. It's better to be like Mary than Martha. While Mary was busy implementing her own ideas of serving Jesus, Mary was busy hearing his word and getting a revelation about what he actually wanted her to do.

Faith is Power

Faith converts God's word into potential spiritual energy. Joshua and Caleb had faith in God's word when he told them to go into the land of Canaan. They believed God would do what he said. For 40 years, they kept believing God in spite of opposition, building up spiritual power through faith that ultimately carried them through the wilderness into the Promised Land. Once there, the power released through their faith overthrew mighty nations and destroyed strong kings.

Step 3. Obedience

The third and final step to operating spiritual technology is obeying the revelation of God. After getting a revelation from God and having faith in it, it's time to act. Whereas faith creates potential spiritual power, obedience releases spiritual power. When faith becomes kinetic or active in the earth, it ultimately unleashes God's kingdom and demolishes Satan's fortresses.

Obedience converts the reality of heaven into an earthly reality. It pivots the word of God from the spiritual realm into the material realm. Obedience causes heaven to rule.

Satan hates obedience to God because he hates the kingdom of God. Satan lies to Christians and says that if they focus too much on obeying Jesus, they'll become legalistic. He tries to discourage them from pursuing hard after obedience to God because he knows if they start obeying God, his dark dominion will be broken.

But obedience to God is not legalism. In reality, obedience is the very definition of Biblical love. "For this is the love of God, that we keep His commandments" (1 John 5:3).

When we obey God, we are actually loving God. We show that we care about him and honor him, and that he is important to us.

"If you love me, keep my commandments. And I will pray the Father, and he will give you another helper, that he may abide with you forever - the Spirit of Truth" (John 14:15-17a). Obeying God is the same as loving God, and it's also connected with being filled with more of the Holy Spirit (Acts 5:32).

Obedience also shows that we know God. "Now by this we know that we know Him, if we keep His commandments" (1 John 2:3). When we do what God says, we show that we are listening to him. He is our Shepherd and we are following him. But when we ignore what Jesus says and do something else, we show that we are following another shepherd instead of the Good Shepherd.

Obedience also reveals that we are abiding in God. "Now he who keeps His commandments abides in Him, and He in him" (1 John 3:24). When we keep Jesus' words, we are under his authority and in close fellowship with him. We are where he wants us to be, doing what he wants us to do.

Obedience shows that we are God's friends. "You are My friends if you do whatever I command you" (John 15:14). God's friends will obey him. His enemies won't.

Obedience is vital. It shows that we love God, know God, abide in God, and are God's friends. And obedience is more than merely a sign of these things; obedience *is* these things.

A touchstone is a hard stone used to determine the genuineness of gold. By drawing the gold across a touchstone, it leaves a streak which reveals whether the gold is pure or not. Obedience is the touchstone of the Christian life, for it proves whether or not our Christian faith is genuine. "But be doers of the word, and not hearers only, deceiving yourselves" (James 1:22). Obedience proves that we have faith in God, because only if we really believe his word will we do what he says. If we don't believe him, we won't. Obedience is therefore the necessary accompaniment to genuine faith.

There is awesome power in obedience. Oswald Chambers said, "When obedience is in the ascendant, He will tax the remotest star and the last grain of sand to assist you with all His Almighty power" (Chambers, *My Utmost for His Highest*). The power that upholds the entire universe is the spiritual power of Almighty God, and this power is released when God's people obey his word.

Obedience to God is the key that opens the door to the miraculous. It is the immediate precursor to a manifestation of God's awesome power and the operation of spiritual technology.

The Pattern for Power

This is the simple three-step pattern to operating spiritual technology.

1. Receive a revelation from God.
2. Believe that revelation, creating potential spiritual power.
3. Obey God, releasing that spiritual power into the earth.

Get revelation through the Holy Spirit, believe it, and obey it. Boom. The kingdom of God comes.

After obeying a specific revelation, we will receive more revelation from God. God gives more light to those who have been faithful with the light they have already been given. "You have been faithful over a few things, I will make you ruler over many things" (Matthew 25:23b).

Oswald Chambers explains:

> All God's revelations are sealed to us until they are
> opened to us by obedience. You will never get them
> open by philosophy or thinking. Immediately you
> obey, a flash of light comes. Let God's truth work in
> you by soaking in it, not by worrying about it. Obey
> God in the thing He is at present showing you, and
> instantly the next thing is opened up. We read tomes
> on the work of the Holy Spirit when... five minutes of
> drastic obedience would make things clear as a sun-
> beam. We say, "I suppose I shall understand these
> things someday." You can understand them now: it is
> not study that does it, but obedience. The tiniest
> fragment of obedience, and heaven opens up and the
> profoundest truths of God are yours straight away.
> God will never reveal more truth about Himself till
> you obey what you know already. Beware of being wise
> and prudent. (Chambers, *My Utmost for His Highest*)

Obedience through faith to a revelation from God is the
Biblical pattern that was followed by men and women of
God throughout history to produce miracles and accom-
plish God's will upon the earth.

"Thus Noah did, according to all that God commanded him, so he did" (Genesis 6:22). Noah heard God, believed him, and built a huge boat that survived a cataclysmic flood. He kept the seeds of creation alive on the top of the waves and birthed a new world.

"Thus Moses did, according to all that the Lord had commanded him, so he did" (Exodus 40:16). Moses heard God, believed his word, and released a nation from bondage in Egypt, bringing them to the border of the Promised Land.

Revelation, faith, and obedience are three spiritual steps that are repeated over and over again throughout the entire Bible. They are the rhythm of how God works throughout history from the beginning of time until now. This is how great men and women of God like Abraham, Isaiah, Mary, Peter, Paul, and many others did amazing works for God and operated spiritual technology.

Fellowship

Finally, to operate spiritual technology, we need each other. Within the body of Christ, the working of the Holy Spirit creates a spiritual sum that is much greater than its individual parts.

The church is being built together "till we all come to the unity of the faith and of the knowledge of the Son of God, to a perfect man, to the measure of the stature of the fullness of Christ" (Ephesians 4:12b-13). God is preparing us to reveal awesome spiritual power and glory together - as a singular MAN made up of many members - all over the world.

When God's people come together in unity, they will fulfill the last prayer of Jesus: "...that they all may be one; as you, Father, are in me, and I in you, that they also may be one in us: that the world may believe that you sent me" (John 17:21). Jesus wants his people to be united, because he knows that when we are, the world will be astounded by a revelation of God.

Behold, how good and pleasant it is
For brethren to dwell together in unity!
It is like precious oil upon the head,
running down on the beard,
The beard of Aaron,
Running down on the edge of his garments.
It is like the dew of Hermon,
Descending on the mountains of Zion.
For there the Lord commanded the blessing -
life forevermore.

(Psalm 133)

Blessing is promised to God's people who dwell together in unity. Unity is like the anointing oil which came down upon the head of the high priest Aaron, equipping him for God's service. Unity brings life, power, and blessing. When God's people come together, they will be supernaturally empowered to accomplish the purposes of God. They will experience the Holy Spirit as the early church did, when they were all "of one heart and of one soul" (Acts 4:32). The end times glory of the united church will be even greater than what was experienced by the early church.

We need to learn the skills of spiritual technology, and we need to operate such skills in submission to our brothers and sisters in the body of Christ. When we do, God's spiritual redemptive power will be revealed, problems will be solved, and the world will be astounded by God.

- RECAP -

1. It is possible for each Christian to operate divine spiritual technology.

2. Both the baptism of the Holy Spirit and obedience to the New Testament are essential to experiencing God's power.

3. To operate spiritual technology, we must first receive a revelation from God.

4. Next, we need to believe that revelation. Faith comes by hearing God speak. Faith creates potential spiritual power.

5. Finally, we must obey that revelation. Obedience releases spiritual power.

6. By implementing the principles of revelation, faith, and obedience in our lives and churches, we can operate spiritual technology.

- PRAYER -

Heavenly Father, I want to hear your voice. Speak to me, Lord. Open my spiritual ears to hear your words and anoint my spiritual eyes so I can see. Deliver me from other voices. Help me wait for you and hear specifically what you want me to do. Deliver me from wasting my time on my own works. Increase my faith in your word and help me believe your word without any doubt.

Help me to always ground my faith on the eternal reality of your word, not my own desires. Help me to obey you so that your kingdom can come through my life. In Jesus' name I pray. Amen.

Chapter 4
Materialism and Cessationism: Rejecting God's Power

When you are arguing against God, you are arguing against the very power that makes you able to argue at all.

C.S. Lewis, *Mere Christianity*

ONE PRIMARY ENEMY of spiritual technology is the ideology of materialism. Materialism teaches that the only things that exist are material things - things that can be seen, touched, and measured. According to materialists, if something is not made of matter, it does not exist. Therefore, stark materialism rejects all things spiritual, including God, because God is a spirit (John 4:24).

Materialism is incompatible with Christianity. Christianity is based on spiritual reality, and a denial of spiritual things undercuts its very foundation. A successful Christian thrives by looking at invisible, immaterial things - and living for those things.

> While we do not look at the things which are seen, but at the things which are not seen. For the things which are seen are temporary, but the things which are not seen are eternal. (2 Corinthians 4:18)

When Christians are influenced by materialism, they doubt spiritual things, and their spiritual lives are hindered. In order to operate spiritual technology (and be effective for God), Christians must reject materialism.

Desperation

There was once a woman who was constantly bleeding, and no one could help her. She had spent all her money on doctors, and her savings were wiped out. She tried the best material technology she could find, and it had failed.

Mark records what happened:

> Now a certain woman had a flow of blood for twelve years, and had suffered many things from many physi-

cians. She had spent all that she had and was no better, but rather grew worse. When she heard about Jesus, she came behind Him in the crowd and touched His garment. For she said, 'If only I may touch His clothes, I shall be made well.' Immediately the fountain of her blood was dried up, and she felt in her body that she was healed of the affliction. (Mark 5:25-29)

When the bleeding woman reached out her hand and touched Jesus' shirt, a surge of spiritual power flashed out from Jesus and entered her body. This power went right to her disease, crushing it. The woman was healed! What the best medical technology could not do for 12 years, Jesus did in an instant! The limitations of material technology— man, money, and materials— were shattered by the power of spiritual technology.

Scientific Blindness

Imagine for a moment if a group of scientists had bustled up to Jesus and hooked up probes to his body, trying to measure the miraculous surge of energy flowing out from him.

Their probes would have found nothing. The powerful spiritual energy emanating from Jesus— the most powerful force in the universe, strong enough to heal the sick and raise the dead— would have registered zero on their charts.

"You have hidden these things from the wise and prudent and have revealed them to babes" (Matt. 11:25b).

The rise of materialism has enthroned science as the world's primary source of truth. Science explains the material world but ignores the spiritual realm, leaving its followers limited. Those who look to science alone to understand the world often reject spiritual things because science says nothing about them.

Scientists have become the world's high priests. Dressed in white lab coats and working away in laboratories, scientists uncover hidden mysteries. When they emerge, they interpret these secrets to the masses, revealing "truth" to the world.

Scientists have become the new agents of world redemption. Out from their laboratories issue forth faster computers, smarter phones, more effective drugs, and other redemptive tools that rescue our world from the evil effects of the Fall.

Yet scientists bumble when faced with the spirit realm. They can't understand it because their materialistic philosophy precludes it, and their methods of investigation are inadequate to analyze it. Probes cannot detect the Holy Spirit. Test tubes cannot measure God. The spiritual realm is completely different than the material realm, and spiritual means are required to understand spiritual things.

God created the universe in 6 days through the spiritual power of his Word, and he upholds the universe until today "by the word of his power" (Hebrews 1:3). God's consistent application of spiritual force preserves the earth, makes scientific laws reliable, and makes scientific research according to repeatable principles possible.

Science is blinded by materialistic presuppositions to the spiritual power that underlies the universe. Ironically, science is blind to the fundamental reality upon which her enterprise rests. Without knowledge of the spiritual realm, science can never truly understand the world.

Material Technology Offers Salvation Without Repentance

When Jesus was here, he put a few conditions on salvation. He basically said, "If you want to be saved, repent. If you want healing, you must come to God in faith. If you want to live forever, trust in me alone. You don't need to pay any money, but you need to hand your life over to God."

Material technology offers redemption without any such conditions. It doesn't care about sin. It doesn't care about faith in God. It can be used by anyone according to their will, as long as they have enough money. This makes material technology popular. People want to be saved from their problems, but they don't want to forsake their sin. They want redemption from difficulties, but they don't want to crucify their flesh. For them, material technology offers the perfect salvation, because it's blind to the wickedness of their hearts. Materialism calls out, "Be saved without Jesus! Be healed, be delivered from depression, live longer, and be happy without God!"

Our source of redemption can have eternal consequences. Take the bleeding woman, for example. If she had been alive today, she probably would have gone to a hospital. After popping a few pills and having a minor surgery, her bleeding would have stopped. In the hospital, she wouldn't have heard about Jesus, and she wouldn't have needed faith. She might have never even thought about God. If she had been healthy and happy when Jesus came to town, she might have just sat at home. Why run out into the street to meet the Savior when everything is fine?

If the bleeding woman had been redeemed by material technology, she may have never found God. It was the insufficiency of material technology that drove her to Christ's feet and sparked the salvation of her soul.

Material technology is not inherently bad, perhaps. But it offers an ultimately empty salvation, for it leaves God out of the picture. Surely it's better to face a few challenges on this earth and be with Christ for eternity, rather than sleep through life on a soft pillow and be thrown into hell forever. Technology might give us all the comforts in the world, but without God, what's the point?

There was a reason Adam was kicked out of the Garden of Eden after his sin. God wanted him to bear sin's painful consequences so he would turn to him for redemption.

Real redemption takes time. It takes time for God's kingdom to grow in the earth. It takes time for the victory of Jesus to be fully revealed. People don't want to wait these days. They want everything fast. Fast food, fast games, fast answers. They want healing now. They want problems solved now. They want utopia now. Basically, they want the evil results of the Fall removed immediately without waiting for God. Material technology compensates for the delayed arrival of the full redemption of the kingdom of God with technological redemption that is according to our own time and according to our own will.

Materialism Easily Disproved by God's Present Power

When Jesus raised up Lazarus from the dead, his enemies were flummoxed. They couldn't deny Christ's power. When God used Peter and John to make a lame man walk, their enemies said, "That a notable miracle has been done through them is evident to all who dwell in Jerusalem, and we cannot deny it" (see Acts 4:16b). Today, when miracles happen, materialists are silent, for miracles disprove materialism as easily as fire disproves non-flammability.

A clear manifestation of the miraculous power of God is the best rebuttal of materialism. The working of the Holy Spirit is the strongest evidence to prove God's present power and reality.

C.H. Spurgeon said:

> The greatest, strongest, mightiest plea for the church of God in the world is the existence of the Spirit of

God in its midst, and the works of the Spirit of God are the true evidences of Christianity.

In order to disprove materialism, the church needs the clear manifestation of the Holy Spirit through specific operations of power. Spiritual technology is the clearest evidence that God is there and that he is active among his people today.

Men and women of God throughout history have recognized that true Christianity is based on spiritual power.

William Carey said:

> However the influence of the Holy Spirit may be set at nought, and run down by many, it will be found upon trial, that all means which we can use, without it, will be ineffectual. (Carey, *Enquiry into the Obligation of Christians...*)

We can try all kinds of things, but without the Holy Spirit, none of it is really going to work. We need spiritual technology to be effective Christians.

Cessationism: The Church Rejects Spiritual Technology

Sadly, many Christians today reject spiritual technology. The church has even developed a theology to justify her unbelief in spiritual things: cessationism. Cessationism is a doctrine that claims God no longer works miracles.

Cessationists say that miracles were fine for Jesus and his apostles, but they aren't for today. Cessationists claim that miracles are great for heaven in the future, but not for today. Cessationists allow a miraculous past and permit a miraculous future, but they disallow a miraculous present.

Interestingly, many cessationists believe that Satan works miracles today, but not God. Cessationists are therefore not strict materialists, for they believe in Satanic miracles, but they believe God's miracles have stopped.

Cessationism is not based on the Bible. Nowhere does the Bible say that God's miracles would stop. As D. Martyn Lloyd-Jones said:

> It is perfectly clear that in New Testament times, the gospel was authenticated in this way by signs, wonders and miracles of various characters and descriptions. . . Was it only meant to be true of the early church? . . .

The Scriptures never anywhere say that these things were only temporary — never! There is no such statement anywhere. (Lloyd-Jones, *The Sovereign Spirit*)

The Bible is replete with miracles, from beginning to end. Everything God does is supernatural, and He's still the same today, working by supernatural means to accomplish His will on the earth. We need to expect the supernatural working of the Holy Spirit among us, because our God is supernatural.

The basis of cessationism is materialism, not good Bible exegesis. In the words of Jonathan Edwards, "we ought not to limit God where He has not limited Himself" (*Edwards on Revival*). If God has not said in His word that spiritual technology would stop, why would we conclude that it has?

This is something the devil would say, in order to tie the hands of the church through the thick cords of unbelief.

False Theologies are Often Based on Experience, Not the Bible

Many cessationists have never experienced spiritual technology themselves, so they conclude that no one else has, either. They aren't willing to believe in something they haven't experienced.

Others have seen the misuse of spiritual gifts, so they deduce that all supposed operations of spiritual gifts must be false. Based on their personal experience (or lack thereof), they conclude that spiritual technology is not for today.

But personal experience is not a stable basis for sound theology. Just because we haven't experienced spiritual technology doesn't mean no one else has. And just because someone has misused spiritual gifts doesn't mean everyone misuses them. People have misused the name of Jesus throughout history, but that doesn't mean we should stop using His name. The Bible has been misused, but we don't throw away the Bible. Spiritual gifts may have been misused, but we shouldn't reject them, especially when the Bible commands us to "earnestly desire" them (1 Corinthians 12:31).

Cessationists actually fall into the same trap they accuse "charismaniacs" of falling into. They base their theology on experience (or lack thereof) rather than on the word of God.

Resisting the Teaching of Being Born Again

It's common for Christians to reject truths that they themselves have never experienced. For example, some "Christians" don't understand the need to be born again. They themselves aren't born again, and they can't imagine that anyone else could be born again either.

These "Christians" confirm their personal experience with bad examples. For example, they might know a person who heard the gospel in a Baptist church, accepted the altar call, and prayed to be born again. Later, this "convert" turned away from God. They conclude, "This born again stuff is a lie. Look at Joe! He said he was born again and now look at his life! He's getting drunk all the time and tells everyone there's no God!"

It's similar with spiritual gifts. Christians who have never experienced the spiritual gifts say, "Look at these crazy people dancing around and speaking in tongues. They go from here and live just like unbelievers. Tongues are not helping them be holy!"

But bad examples do not disprove the truth. Instead, they show that Satan counterfeits the truth in order to deceive people and give the truth a bad name.

Christian Confusion

God's way of convincing the world is through the "demonstration of the Spirit and power" (1 Corinthians 2:4). Cessationist churches refuse to operate spiritual technology, and this is one reason why they have difficulty convincing the world there is a God. Without a demonstration of power, they must come up with other means to try to convince people.

They send out "apologists" who try to convince people of the truth of Christianity using intellectual arguments. Sadly, these "apologies" rarely seem to win souls for Christ. The church's real problem is not a lack of good arguments, but a lack of spiritual power. The absence of genuine spiritual power is the primary reason why materialism is able to lie and tell the world there is no God. When God shows up and his power is revealed, a materialist world (along with an impotent church) will have to stop arguing.

Not all Christian denominations are cessationist, of course. Some Pentecostal and Charismatic churches believe in the present working of God's power. But the miracles that happen among these groups often seem confusing - gold dust, flying gemstones, and psychosomatic healing of mysterious pain. "If the trumpet makes an uncertain sound, who will prepare for battle?" (1 Corinthians 14:8).

Some charismatic Christians lie on the floor, "slain in the Spirit" and "soaking in God." When they get up, they bark like dogs, crow like roosters, or laugh uncontrollably. This behavior is not helpful. Some of these manifestations may be demonic.

Some churches fall into the ditch of charismania, and others fall into the ditch of cessationism. Both of these ditches are tools Satan uses to trip up the church and deviate her from achieving her glorious goal. We need the real power of God, not a Satanic counterfeit. We also need a living God, not dead Christianity that is devoid of God's Spirit.

Material Technology Seems More Reliable

In the meantime, while part of the church embraces lying miracles and another part of the church fights against God, material technology races ahead, offering increasing redemption in more areas of life. Modern medicine heals more and more diseases. Travel becomes easier and more accessible. Communication becomes faster and more lifelike.

To most people today, material technology seems to work, whereas spiritual technology doesn't. Science gives answers, but religion creates problems. Materialism is a fact, God is a myth. When most people face problems, they run to the hospital, psychologist, government, or to the internet - anywhere but the church. This is not the fault of desperate people. It's the fault of a powerless church.

Without spiritual technology, the church focuses on the future rather than on the present. She tells people of the glories of heaven and hands out free tickets to get there, promising that it is possible to escape current trouble mainly by dying and going to be with God. But by focusing on future glory instead of what is presently possible, the church abdicates her calling to be the single most powerful agent of redemptive change in the world. Living in the future, rather than the present, renders the church irrelevant.

The End of Cessationism and the Rise of the Church

The Bible says that before Jesus returns, the church will be glorious and powerful, reflecting the light of her husband, Jesus - "a glorious church, not having spot or wrinkle or any such thing, but... holy and without blemish" (Ephesians 5:27). This prophetic declaration controls the future destiny of the church.

The Bible says that God is "the same yesterday, today, and forever" (Hebrews 13:8). In the beginning, God created the world by spiritual power - speaking light, matter, and natural laws into existence. At the end of the age, God is going to judge the world, and this present age will end in an awesome flash of God's glory. Everything that happens between these two spectacular bookends of world history is full of God's miracles. God's spiritual power surrounds us, even though we can't see it. The continuation and order of the universe is one huge miracle, a massive testimony to God's great wisdom and power! We need to open our eyes to the rich spiritual reality that surrounds us.

The kingdom of God is coming, and nothing can stop it. It's coming through holy people, not faster computers. It's coming through the power of the Holy Spirit, not through material technology. A remnant of the church will soon rise out of the twin demonic ditches of charismania and cessationism, and get back to the pure word of God. She will become the glorious and spotless bride of Christ. She will release the kingdom of God into the world by spiritual power. God bought redemption for the world at the infinite cost of the life of his Son, and he's going to redeem it through the operations of the Holy Spirit. His Son did not die in vain.

When the church awakes, she will operate spiritual technology all over the world, and the glory of the Lord will be revealed. "The glory of the LORD shall be revealed, And all flesh shall see it together; For the mouth of the LORD has spoken" (Isaiah 40:5).

When this happens, materialism will be stripped off the eyes of the world like a veil from a face, and the earth will be rescued from the thrall of Satan, the dark spiritual being who stands behind the lie of materialism.

- RECAP -

1. Materialism is the belief that the spiritual realm is not real and that the only real things are comprised of matter.

2. Materialism is a controlling philosophy of the modern age. It is an ideological enemy of spiritual technology.

3. Material technology offers technology redemption in many areas of life, but it is an ultimately empty salvation, because it offers redemption without God.

4. Cessationism is Christian materialism.

5. Materialism is disproved by the operating of divine spiritual power.

6. The church is not consistently operating in spiritual technology, which leaves a redemptive void that is filled by material technology.

7. The church will someday be filled with the Holy Spirit and reveal divine spiritual power to the world.

- PRAYER -

Heavenly Father, thank you for the material tools that help me, but I know that I need your Holy Spirit to bring true redemption in any situation. Help me touch you in faith like the bleeding woman did, so that I can experience your saving power in more and more areas of my life. Deliver me from all wrong ways of thinking that hinder me from believing in your word. Increase my faith in what is possible through Jesus. I want to operate in spiritual technology. I reject all forms of cessationism. I believe there is no limitation with you. Awaken me so that I can fulfill your miraculous purposes. In Jesus' name I pray. Amen.

Chapter 5
Surviving and Winning in the Last Days

Blessed be God, that we live in these latter times - the latter times of the reign of darkness and imposture. Great is our privilege, precious our opportunity, to cooperate with the Saviour in the blessed work of enlarging and establishing his kingdom throughout the world.

Adoniram Judson

AT THE END of the age, thick spiritual darkness is going to cover the world like a cloak. People will become disillusioned with the empty promises of materialism and discover that material technology is unable to solve their ultimate problems. They will become spiritually hungry.

Seeking spiritual experiences, many of them will be attracted to dark spiritual forces.

Witchcraft is the use of demonic spiritual energy to manipulate the world, and it's already becoming popular. Wicca is a modern name for witchcraft, and according to some sources, it is among the fastest-growing religions in North America. Witches often claim that they are manipulating the world through positive spiritual energy, but in reality, they are using demonic forces. Any use of spiritual energy to manipulate the world apart from the true God is witchcraft.

Children's books like Harry Potter are introducing children to witchcraft. Harry Potter and his young friends attend a school called *Hogwarts School of Witchcraft and Wizardry* so they can learn how to cast spells and engage in demonic rituals. These fictional characters are the role models of a new generation.

Witchcraft operates by engaging and releasing the power of evil spirits. Rituals engage demons by using symbols, altars, candles, chants, sacrifices, and sins. These tools are employed in specific arrangements, times, and places in order to harness demonic energy and direct it toward people or situations and gain desired outcomes.

Demons and fallen angels are the spiritual power behind all witchcraft. Evil spirits work miracles according to the will of people in exchange for those people's souls. This dark exchange promises spiritual power without submission to God. "Do what thou wilt" is the command that underlies modern forms of witchcraft and Satanism. Demons are willing to do what people want as long as they can drag them into hell.

Popularizing the Occult

Satan has come out of the shadows in today's culture, and he's making a brazen last attempt to attract people. Heavy metal bands pour out demonic lyrics and employ Satanic symbols on stage. Television shows seek to normalize witchcraft. Video games are full of occult imagery and dark spirituality.

Increasing numbers of people are attracted to the devil because they are hungry for spiritual reality, and they aren't finding it in many churches. Satan is a real spirit with plenty of power; he's just very evil. When the church doesn't operate spiritual technology as God intended, there is a void. Satan jumps in to fill this void with his own counterfeit spirituality, and spiritually hungry people get excited.

Satan is no joke. He's not entertainment. He's not a cool guy who can help us get things done. He's a liar, a brutal tormenter, and a ruthless murderer. Soon he, along with all his legions of demons and fallen angels, will be consigned to the lake of fire forever. All his human followers are going to end up in eternal fire along with him. Some of them thought that serving the devil would be a fun way to get power in this world, so they sold their souls to him for a few temporary perks. When they reach the hot fires of hell, they will be shocked to discover that they have been damned forever in exchange for a few worthless trinkets.

Witchcraft and Satanism are weak and foolish novelties. Jesus Christ has crushed Satan's skull and destroyed every demon. The name of Jesus has the power to break every curse and disrupt any witchcraft. There is no spiritual match for Jesus Christ, the Son of God. Don't waste your life on the devil. If you want to really impact the world, renounce Satan, trust in Jesus, and work for God's glorious kingdom.

Deception in the Church

The church holds the key to Satan's final demise, and Satan knows it. If he can infiltrate the church, he can delay his own downfall. Satan works hard to deceive the church, and he is preparing to unleash a strong deception in the end times that will swamp many Christians (see Matthew 7:21-23; 2 Thessalonians 2:3; Jude; 2 Peter; and 1 John 3).

Satan has many tricks up his sleeve. False Christian teachers spread doctrinal error. Man-made religious traditions cause people to engage in religious activity that is not based on the word of God (anytime we engage in religious activity that is not based on the word of God, we potentially open ourselves up to demonic spirits).

Lying miracles deceive many Christians. Lying miracles lie about their spiritual origin; they claim to be from Jesus but are actually from Satan. Those who work lying miracles say (and usually believe) that they are working miracles by the Holy Spirit. But they are deceived (2 Thessalonians 2:9). Lying miracles can spawn false "Christian" revivals which are replete with demonic power and manifestations of evil spirits.

"For false christs and false prophets will rise and show great signs and wonders to deceive, if possible, even the elect" (Matthew 24:24)."

Discernment

We need to be careful when dealing with spiritual forces. There are many evil spirits in this world seeking to trick

Christians, and they often operate within the church. Just because a miracle happens in the church by a "Christian" minister doesn't mean that the Holy Spirit is behind it. It could be the devil working a miracle.

We don't need to be paranoid and look for Satan everywhere, but we need to recognize that both God and Satan can work miracles within the church. This will help protect us from the extremes of cessationism on one hand ("God doesn't work miracles today") and charismania on the other ("all miracles in the church must be from God"). We need to avoid both of these extremes in order to be effective Christians. We need to mature and learn how to tell the difference between miracles from God and miracles from Satan within the church.

We must test the spirits.

"Beloved, do not believe every spirit, but test the spirits, whether they are of God; because many false prophets have gone out into the world" (1 John 4:1).

Each Christian has a responsibility to test the spiritual source of any miracle that he sees. Miracles come from spirits, and spirits work through people, so when the person is tested, the spirit behind the miracle is tested.

The Bible tells us how to test a miracle-worker: "No one can say that Jesus is Lord except by the Holy Spirit" (1 Corinthians 12:3b).

This simple test tells us that if a miracle-worker confesses that Jesus is Lord, then he is operating by the Holy Spirit, but if he doesn't confess that Jesus is Lord, he's working miracles by an evil spirit. Confessing that "Jesus is Lord" means more than repeating those exact words. When Jesus is the Lord of someone's life, that person will obey Jesus. The Holy Spirit will lead him to submit to the commands of the New Testament and abandon the religious traditions of men. Miracle workers who are inspired by the Holy Spirit will teach and practice the word of God. On the other hand, lying spirits lead people away from the word of God into man-made religious practices, and false miracle workers will ignore teachings of the New Testament. Through this test, we can discern whether the spirit operating miracles through a person is the Holy Spirit or an evil spirit.

Confidence in God

There will be a lot of confusing spiritual activity in the end times, and we will need more and more of the Holy Spirit to keep us safe and strong. The more of the Holy Spirit we have, the more equipped we will be to face these spiritual challenges. If we ask God for more of the Holy Spirit, he will give him to us.

> If a son shall ask bread of any of you that is a father, will he give him a stone? Or if he ask a fish, will he for a fish give him a serpent? Or if he shall ask an egg, will he offer him a scorpion? If you then, being evil, know how to give good gifts unto your children: how much more shall your heavenly Father give the Holy Spirit to them that ask him? (Luke 11:11-13)

We can confidently ask God to fill us with his Spirit, knowing that he will not fill us with an evil spirit instead.

Dangerous Technologies

In the end times, as spiritual darkness rises, evil uses of material technology will also rise. Technological tools that have been used to solve human problems, like the internet and digital payment systems, will morph into tools of Satanic bondage. Powerful systems of surveillance will be created, eliminating privacy. These systems will become ubiquitous, and those shut out of these systems will be shut out of the world economy. Artificial intelligence and robotics will further enmesh humanity in a global spider's web.

Material technology will culminate with the Mark of the Beast - technology implanted in the hand or head, without which no one will be able to buy or sell (Revelation 13:17). This Mark will create a worldwide economic system that will rest in the hands of the Antichrist. Christians are commanded by God to refuse the Mark of the Beast. When they reject this Mark, they will be shut out of the world economy and be unable to buy or sell. How will they survive in this time? The only answer is spiritual technology.

Great Tribulation

Corrie Ten Boom was a godly woman who was imprisoned by the Nazis in Germany. When she was asked about when the great tribulation would arrive, she replied, "It's already here." She knew firsthand that God's people will have trouble in this world (John 16:33), and she always encouraged Christians to be prepared.

Persecution under the Nazis was bad, but it's going to get worse at the end of the age. Jesus described conditions on the earth at the end of time this way: "For then there will be great tribulation, such as has not been since the beginning of the world until this time, no, nor ever shall be" (Matthew 24:21).

Christians are going to need to know how to survive the great tribulation. They will need to eat food, drink water, get clothes and shelter, survive disease, and be protected.

The Only Way to Survive

Survivalist practices like stocking up on food, getting farmland, and having a source of water might help. But ultimately, these natural means of preparation will be limited. Food will run out, and farms may be confiscated.

Material technology won't help much either. Internet, smartphones, cars - all of these will become useless for Christians who are shut out of the world economy. Money, guns, bombs, armies, politics - none of this will help. There will be terrible diseases that no medicine can cure, powerful weaponry that will subdue any militia, and dangerous robots that are impervious to human attack. Only God will be able to resolve these challenges, and we need the Holy Spirit to help us.

Christians will be in the midst of the greatest challenges the world has ever faced, and they won't be able to buy food at the grocery store, fill up their cars with gas, or buy electricity. The solution is not death. The solution is appropriating the power of God. The only way for Christians to survive will be through the miraculous power of

God. They will need to consistently operate spiritual technology in order to experience miraculous provision from God.

Just like in the Bible, the saints of God in the end times are going to have to learn to live by the supernatural power of God. Physical healing will come through the Holy Spirit. Provision will come from heaven, just as when Jesus multiplied bread and fish. The Holy Spirit will transport the children of God where they need to go, just as he transported Philip. The power of God will be revealed against God's enemies, rendering guns and bombs useless against God's children.

The Impending Light

As God's people operate spiritual technology in the midst of great tribulation, spiritual light will shine that will provide all that God's children need to keep them safe in the midst of the greatest storm the world has ever seen. God's power will keep them safe and protect them. Through them, the spiritual power of God will shine. Isaiah prophesied:

Arise, shine, for your light has come, and the glory of the Lord is risen upon you. For behold, the darkness shall cover the earth, and deep darkness the people;

but the Lord shall arise over you, and his glory will be seen upon you. The Gentiles shall come to your light, and kings to the brightness of your rising. (Isaiah 60:1-3)

In the midst of thick darkness, God's light will shine. This spiritual light from God won't shine as a light in the atmosphere or some sort of spiritual bolt out of the blue, but as spiritual power in and through God's people. This spiritual light will specifically manifest as spiritual technology operating through God's people, releasing the glory and power of God into the world.

A new day is coming. All the strength of the world and the flesh will melt away. The spiritual power of God will remain. True Christians will be conquerors amidst the rubble of the end times. Everyone is going to see it. Nations will stand in awe.

Corporate Preparation

God has a rich spiritual land for his people to enter into, replete with powerful operations of spiritual technology for the full defeat of Satan and the total deliverance of the world from all effects of the Fall. We as God's children must enter into this inheritance together and partake of its riches corporately in order to reveal God's glorious victory to the world.

Christians in the end times will enter their divine inheritance together. Only together can we face the challenges of the end times successfully. We need to learn to submit to each other and to follow Jesus together. There is protection, power, and blessing when believers are united under Jesus.

We must revolutionize our understanding of how God wants his church to be. Only the church as it's defined by God will be able to fulfill its divine purpose. We must get back to church as God intended, if we want to operate in spiritual technology as God has planned. The radical, New Testament, Acts 2 and 4 church is our goal. We must see the bride of Christ raised up in the earth, patterned according to the word of God.

Church is not to be an occasional meeting; it's to be a lifestyle. We must gather together into house church communities that are interconnected with other such communities, share our possessions and lives, showing each other and the world the love of Jesus. When we begin to raise up an alternative society, bearing each other's burdens and living as the body of Christ on the earth, we will be preparing for survival, just as Noah prepared an ark that would survive the great flood. The true church will be like an ark or a place to find refuge from the Satanic storm that is going to ravage the world.

This powerful community won't happen easily. It wasn't easy for Noah to build a huge boat while everyone else was looking on, mocking. The risks for such an endeavor may seem enormous. It's never easy to step outside the boundaries of what is considered normal and do something different than everyone else. But that's okay. Nothing that is truly valuable is easy. Considering the impending arrival of the Antichrist, the Great Tribulation, and the Mark of the Beast, we might as well go for it because we don't have anything to lose.

Body of Christ on the Earth

When the bride of Christ is revealed, she will become the womb through which the deliverance of God is manifested to the world. Jesus completely transformed cities in ancient Israel through spiritual power. Soon his people will transform the world through the same spiritual power.

We are the body of Christ on the earth (1 Corinthians 12:12). We are members of Jesus' flesh and bones (Ephesians 5:30). We are his bride that is called to represent him to the world. Imagine what would happen if Jesus' body actually lived out its calling to be a large group of unified people all over the world, all of whom are in touch with the Father, all of whom are filled with the Holy Spirit, all of whom are doing the awesome works of God. They would move in synchrony all over the world, swamping it with God's light and power.

Imagine Jesus' works being done everywhere, his words being spoken all over the world. Imagine the glory of God penetrating all the dark corners of the earth. Such an astounding revelation of Christ will swamp the world and completely transform it. This is God's plan.

God is raising up people who will listen to his voice and submit to him. They will walk according to the impulses of the Holy Spirit, not relying on the systems of the world but on God. Their interactions with the world will be controlled by revelations from their Father.

At the end of the age, mature believers will become what God intended humans to be from the creation of the world. They will recover, through Jesus, the fullness of what Adam lost. They will walk in divine spiritual authority and utilize the full range of spiritual technology, carrying spiritual dominance over the world.

God's people will become far more capable than the most advanced cyborg, robot, or sorcerer. Their power will be a holy spiritual force, based on God's life. They will submit to God and be willing to lay down their own lives. They will not be their own "little gods," doing their own thing according to their own will, but they will be God's obedient sons who represent their Father accurately to the world.

"The earnest expectation of the creation eagerly waits for the revealing of the sons of God" (Romans 8:19).

Ever since the Fall, the creation has been groaning under the bondage of sin and death. The plants and animals are struggling under the curse, waiting for the sons of God to rise up and reveal God's light and glory into the world. Jesus has already paid the price for the redemption of the creation, and now he's waiting for us to grow into spiritual maturity and become the people God has called us to be.

"The creation itself also shall be delivered from the bondage of corruption into the glorious liberty of the children of God" (Romans 8:21).

Spiritual Technology Will Set the Creation Free

God created the earth to glorify himself, and someday she will fulfill this lofty purpose. Praise will resound from the mountains. The valleys will shout God's glory. The trees, plants, and animals will all be set free from decay and death and radiate praise back to God. Eden will be restored to the world (Isaiah 11:6; 55:13). The creation will fulfill the purpose for which it was made, which is to glorify Almighty God.

Through the operation of spiritual technology, the glory of God will crash over the world in astounding, overwhelming measure. Sin, Satan, sickness, decay, wars, death - everything that is wrong in the world - will be eliminated by the glorious triumph of Christ in and through his people.

"The earth will be filled with the knowledge of the glory of the Lord as the waters cover the sea" (Habakkuk 2:14).

In that day there will be no more problems. There will be no more conflict, pain, sorrow, or tears. There will be no more hunger, poverty, disease, or death. The great goals of God's redemptive plan in Christ will be accomplished, and Jesus will reign over the earth as king of kings. Spiritual technology will have manifested the fullness of the kingdom of God.

Material Technology Will Pass Away

In that day, material technology will pass away. Material technology will have no more reason to exist because there will be no problems. If food is abundant on every tree, tractors and plows are not needed. If weather is perfect, central heating and cooling are not required. Perfect health will eliminate the need for medical technology. The internet will become superfluous when the Holy Spirit reveals all secrets. Cars and airplanes will be unnecessary when God takes us where we need to go.

In the fullness of the kingdom of God, there will be no computers, no hospitals, no antidepressants, no guns, no smartphones, no cars. God and his perfect spiritual technology will be all that is needed. In the fullness of the kingdom of God, all forms of material technology will pass away, made as irrelevant as a flashlight by the bright noonday sun.

Spiritual technology, on the other hand, will last forever, because throughout eternity the Holy Spirit will reveal God's glory in ever-increasing measure, enforcing divine order throughout the creation through the spiritual operations of his power.

Time to Act

Considering the glorious goal of God for the world and the fact that God has given us spiritual technology to accomplish this goal, it's time to act. We are the body of Christ on the earth. We are his representatives in this world. Christ's way must become our way. His miracles must become our miracles. His authority must become our authority. We need to know what it means to speak and act in Jesus' name, stamping our words and works with the authority of Christ. Let's not be daunted by the apparent impossibility of it all. With God, all things are possible.

Look to God. The world needs apostles of Christ, not humanoid robots. We need wisdom from the Holy Spirit, not faster laptops. We need spiritual power, not a better internet connection. Jesus is waiting for us, more than we're waiting for him.

As we prepare to be entrusted with the powerful spiritual technology of God, we will have to go through experiences we don't understand. God is training us. He's teaching us to be sensitive to his voice, showing us the dangers of disobedience and the blessings of obedience. He's teaching us spiritual precision, preparing us to be vessels he can entrust with his awesome spiritual technology, who will use it only as he directs.

When his people are ready, spiritual technology will operate through the church everywhere, preparing the way for Jesus to return to the earth.

- RECAP -

1. In the end times, spiritual darkness will be thicker than any other time in history.

2. Material technology will continue to develop exponentially. The pinnacle of this emerging technological society will be the Mark of the Beast with the Antichrist at the apex.

3. Dark spiritual forces such as witchcraft and lying miracles will increase, as Satan energizes evil spirits in a final onslaught against humanity.

4. The people of God will face terrible persecution. But the darkness will not overcome the light.

5. When the church comes together in the ways God originally intended, she will be revealed as the bride of Christ.

6. Someday God's people will operate in the full complement of spiritual technology, setting the creation free.

7. At the end of the age, Eden will be restored to the earth, and material technology will be unnecessary.

- PRAYER -

Dear God, Thank you that Jesus defeated all of the forces of darkness on the cross and crushed the head of Satan. Thank you that in Jesus Christ I am more than a conqueror. Help me to always remember that you are greater than all the forces of evil, for you have already overcome them. And as the darkness increases, help me to keep my eyes fixed on you.

I dedicate the rest of my life to you. Whatever you want me to do is what I want to do. There are many changes happening in the world; please help me to get ready for what is coming. Deliver me from the spirit of fear, and fill me with the spirit of power. Give me wisdom. Help me make the decisions I need to make. Connect me with others who long to see your kingdom come. Make me a part of your bride and fill me with your Spirit. In Jesus' name I pray. Amen.

Contact

Visit

www.bethelcornerstone.org

More books by Peter John Brooks:

7 Foundations

Kingdom Explosion

Three Marys

The Coming Glory

Goat Tags

Absurd Christianity